CHAKRA VYUGAM

Lessons from Life's Inner Battles

BY THE SAME AUTHOR

My Gratitude Journal – Everyday Thankfulness

-Deepiga S

Cover design by Deepiga S

ISBN: 979-8897443765

First Edition: 2025

Country of Origin: India

For inquiries contact: Instagram - @inked_with_optimism

Index

Acknowledgement

As I pen the closing words of this journey, my heart swells with gratitude for the countless souls, moments, and places that have shaped Chakra Vyugam - Lessons from Life's Inner Battle.

First and foremost, to my mother – the eternal pillar of my existence, my first teacher, and my constant sanctuary. Your unwavering love and wisdom have been my guiding light in the darkest labyrinths of life. Every lesson you imparted, every sacrifice you made, echoes through the pages of this book.

To my brother – my confidant, my companion in both joy and challenges, and the silent strength I've always leaned on. Your unwavering support and belief in me have been a source of immense courage. You've been both a partner in laughter and a co-warrior in life's battles.

To my friends – the ones who stood steadfast through storms and celebrated my every triumph, big or small. You have been my mirrors, and my cheerleaders. This book would not have been possible without the laughter, tears, and profound insights you shared.

To the people who appeared, often unexpectedly, at different crossroads of my life – some as blessings, others as challenges, and many as teachers in disguise. You may not know the depth of your impact, but each of you has contributed a verse to my story.

To the places that cradled me, inspired me, or even tested me – the quiet corners, the bustling cities, the tranquil landscapes. You've been my sanctuary, my muse, and my battlefield.

To my teachers – thank you for your patience, your knowledge, and your ability to see potential in me where I saw none. You taught me not only lessons for the mind but also for the spirit, planting seeds of courage and curiosity that bore fruit in these pages.

Finally, to life itself – for the mysteries, the battles, and the revelations that make every moment a lesson, every challenge a teacher. This book is my humble attempt to capture the beauty of this inner journey and share it with the world.

To all of you, who has been a part of this story in ways big and small, visible and invisible, thank you from the depths of my soul. This is as much your book as it is mine.

With profound gratitude,

Deepiga S

Chapter 1

Introduction

Chakra Vyugam – a term that conjures images of intricate, ever turning wheels within our lives. In many ways, it feels like the perfect metaphor for the layers of our experiences, our emotions, and our life lessons. As like a warrior caught in a cycle, we find ourselves in these spinning, highly complicated formations of life, each layer represents all areas of our life which are career, relationships, education, money, health and materials. Each layer revealing more about who we are, what drives us, and where we are ultimately headed.

All the life's bitter experiences and the lessons from them don't come neatly packaged. They unfold, often painfully, in layers, and sometimes they hit us only when we're ready to understand them.

Just imagine each chakra—or wheel—as a stage in this complex formation, demanding courage, introspection, and growth. Much like Arjuna (In Mahabharata) facing the endless cycles of his inner conflict, we, too, wrestle with our desires, fears, and responsibilities.

Initially, it feels chaotic, as if we're trapped in a maze with no exit, with every turn revealing yet another challenge, another test. But over time, if we allow ourselves to be present, to observe, and, crucially, to adapt, we come to see the hidden patterns. It's as if the universe unfolds a blueprint for us, with each chakra showing us a facet of ourselves we hadn't seen before.

In my own life, each pivotal moment has been a chakra—an experience that forced me to confront the truth of my own existence. As a young adult, I sought freedom in everything: work, relationships, identity. I wanted to break free from the societal 'vyugam'—the trap of expectations. But as I moved forward, each 'chakra' I encountered made me realize that freedom itself is a delicate balance. True freedom comes not in breaking away, but in understanding and working within the web of responsibilities, choices, and inevitable struggles that define us.

One particular lesson stands out: the realization that not every chakra can or should be conquered. Some are meant to be understood, respected, and moved through. In the spiritual sense, not all energies need to be mastered; some must simply be integrated. When I tried to force control over my experiences, the chakra spun harder, binding me more tightly in the vyugam. Only when I released my grip did I understand that sometimes, the path forward is surrender.

Chakra Vyugam is not just a philosophical journey; it's a survival guide for the spirit. The deeper you go, the more you see that the chakras within us are not only challenges but also sources of power and wisdom. They reveal the ways in which we might conquer ourselves—not by defeating the external, but by understanding the internal.

As I'm writing this, my intention is not merely to share my life lessons but to encourage you, the reader, to view your own struggles as chapters in the vyugam of life. If we embrace them, they become less like traps and more like guides, each one turning us closer to our true selves.

Chapter 2

Chakra 1 – Confronting Fear

This chapter discuss about the initial layers of fear that we encounter in our life's journey, such as fear of failure, disappointing others, and of the unknown. Also, the personal experiences where fear acted as a barrier and how to get through it to unlock the growth is detailed here.

The first chakra of our life is fear. Most of us are deeply trapped into the wheel of fear and gripped by it.

Fear plays a vital role in all areas of life.

1. Preparing for an exam brings the anxiety of potential results.
2. Getting an interview call from a leading organization sparks nervousness about facing the panel.
3. Embarking on a new business venture comes with worries of financial loss or accumulating debts.
4. Embracing family life involves concerns about managing relationships effectively.
5. Exercising for fitness carries the apprehension of enduring physical discomfort.
6. Cooking in the kitchen includes the fear of mishaps like a pressure cooker explosion.

7. Seizing an opportunity often comes with uncertainty about the outcome.
8. Expressing love and affection can evoke fear of how it will be received.
9. Asserting your valid points can bring the worry of whether they'll be acknowledged.
10. Visiting a doctor for an illness brings anxiety about injections and medications.

During my teenage years, I was an avid pet lover and cherished the companionship of a Pomeranian puppy that eventually gave birth to five adorable puppies. All of them appeared healthy and vibrant, except for the last one. Shortly after the delivery, we called a veterinarian to our home to examine the newborns and administer the necessary vaccinations. When the doctor arrived and assessed the puppies, he delivered distressing news: the youngest pup was extremely weak and unlikely to survive more than six to ten hours. He explained that, in many cases, the last-born struggles the most and often succumbs to its frailty.

Hearing this broke my heart. I was terrified at the thought of losing the little one and immediately asked the doctor if there was any way to save it. He explained that caring for such a fragile puppy would require constant vigilance. The pup, being too weak to nurse from its mother, would need to be fed milk using ink filler. It would also need to be kept under controlled warmth, preferably in an incubator, and its heartbeat would have to be closely monitored. Despite his suggestions, the doctor was not optimistic about the puppy's survival.

I was overwhelmed with worry but resolute in my decision to fight for the pup's life. This was my first experience dealing with such a delicate situation, and I couldn't bear the thought of giving up. I devoted myself entirely to the task, staying by the puppy's side without a moment's rest. I fed it milk through the ink filler, placed it on a cozy pillow to keep it warm, and kept a constant watch on its heartbeat. Whenever its heart rate seemed to drop, I gently patted its chest, which miraculously brought it back each time.

Throughout the night and into the next morning, I repeated this routine tirelessly. Despite my efforts and unwavering determination, the puppy showed no signs of improvement. Finally, as the doctor had predicted, the little one passed away. Losing it was a deeply heart-breaking experience, and I felt an immense sense of helplessness knowing I couldn't save it despite all I had done.

This incident, though seemingly simple to some, was profoundly personal to me. It wasn't just about the loss of a pet—it was about grappling with fear, attachment, and the fragility of life. While it was devastating, it also became a moment of growth for me. I learned to face my fears, accept loss, and recognize that some things are beyond our control. This painful experience taught me to perceive life with greater humility and resilience, shaping the way I approach challenges and uncertainties.

No matter how big or small. We often have fears which are unwanted that traps us in all the way possible. Most of us are very keen on not to express out the fear that we battle inside us which is fine, but not acknowledging it doesn't do any good to us and our growth. Confront it wholeheartedly. Acknowledging your fear brings clarity, and it helps to transform your uncertainty into an opportunity to grow.

This eventually cultivates courage, and push you rise above limitations, embracing growth and stepping boldly into a future of endless possibilities.

Practical Steps to Overcome Fear:

Step 1: Journaling: Write down your biggest fears of life. For each fear, ask yourself,

- What is the root cause of this fear?
- What would happen if I faced it?

Writing down your fears allows you to dismantle their power over you. When you confront them, you reveal their true nature – often less daunting than imagined. Also, it's not about eliminating them; it's about learning their origins and impact.

Step 2: Visualization: Close your eyes and imagine yourself facing a fear in a safe space. Picture yourself succeeding in overcoming it.

Fear is a natural response, but unchecked, it can paralyze. When you take time to explore why you feel afraid, you empower yourself to make informed decisions rather than reacting impulsively.

Step 3: Affirmation: Repeat everyday as much as possible "I am stronger than my fears, and I grow by facing them".

 Affirming this positive note everyday builds courage that doesn't mean fearlessness. It means moving forward despite fear. This cultivates strength, gaining the ability to face life's uncertainties with a brave heart. Repeating the positive note, reprogramming our subconscious brain to unlock the door to progress, transforming hesitation into unstoppable momentum.

Spin continues......

Chapter 3

Chakra 2 – The Desire (Balancing Wants and Needs)

This chapter examines the "chakra" of desire, where we confront our ambitions, material desires, and the longing for validation. It includes stories about the consequences of chasing external validation and lessons learned from refocusing on personal values.

Often we get confused over want and need as we progress in each stage of our life.

S.no	Need	Want
1	A need is something essential for survival or basic functioning like food, water, shelter and healthcare.	A want is something you desire but is not essential for survival like luxury items, entertainment, or trendy clothing.
2	Needs are prioritized because they are critical for life and well-being.	Wants are secondary and are pursued after fulfilling needs.
3	Un-fulfilling needs can lead to physical, mental or emotional harm. Example: Lack of food can lead to starvation.	Un-Fulfilling wants may cause dissatisfaction but doesn't threaten survival.

| 4 | Needs are often the focus of essential budgeting and spending. | Wants are discretionary expenses and can be postponed or avoided. |
| 5 | Example: Food, Clean Water, Basic Clothing, Shelter and Education. | Example: Designer Clothes, Fancy Meals, Video games or Vacations. |

The wheel of desire symbolizes the intricate interplay between our ambitions, material cravings, and the longing for external validation. It is a space where many of us lose ourselves in the pursuit of more – more recognition, more wealth, and more approval – only to find a void within.

In my experience, I've observed a story of a mid-level manager who prided himself in his rising status. He dreamed of the day he would be recognized as successful by society. He bought a luxurious apartment and a high-end- car, fuelled by applause of his peers. However, the reality was far less glamorous. Late at night, as he sat in his plush living room, the emptiness grew louder. He realized he wasn't happy. He had neglected meaningful connections, his health, and his love for music – a passion he had buried under corporate deadlines.

One day, his daughter innocently asked "Why are you always tired, dad"? The question broke him and he began re-evaluating his life. He started to learn and practice music again, not for recognition, but for joy. He learned to set boundaries at work, reconnect with his family, friends and spend time on things that truly mattered.

Finally he realized that external validations were fleeting, while internal fulfilment was enduring.

The manager's journey is one many can relate to. We often chase the illusion of happiness through material success, unaware that the price we pay maybe our peace and authenticity. His story reminds us to re-align with personal values. Seeking contentment not in what the world applauds but in what our soul truly craves.

Practical Steps to evaluate fleeting desires over meaningful goals:

Step 1: Reflection Exercise: List your desires in 3 main categories. Example;

    a.   Material (Example: Money, Possessions)
    b.   Emotional (Example: Love, Recognition)
    c.   Spiritual (Example: Peace, Purpose)

Step 2: For each category ask yourself: Does this desire align your value?

Step 3: Everyday Mindfulness: Before pursuing a desire, pause and ask yourself: Is this a need or a want? Will this bring lasting fulfilment?

I believe, these steps greatly assist you to tackle the chakra 2.

Spin continues……

Chapter 4

Chakra 3 – The Responsibility (Duties and Boundaries)

This chapter focuses on the vyugam of an individual's responsibilities exploring how they can either liberate or trap us, depending on our mind set. It also narrates personal experiences of learning to set boundaries while maintaining commitments to family, work, friends and self.

During the mid-point of my career, I encountered one of the most challenging phases of my life: balancing the responsibility of saving my mother's life while managing the demands of a high-pressure career. My mother fell gravely ill and had to be admitted to the hospital. As the eldest child and the primary breadwinner of the family, the weight of responsibility rested solely on my shoulders. I had no guidance or support to lean on, and the uncertainty of whether I could save her made the situation even more harrowing.

Simultaneously, my professional responsibilities were at their peak. I held a critical role that required me to manage operations across multiple global regions, often spanning different time zones. Taking leave was not an option, and I found myself caught in an exhausting cycle of attending to my mother's health while fulfilling the relentless demands of my job.

Adding to the complexity, I refrained from seeking help from friends or relatives. It stemmed from my inherent belief that I shouldn't be a burden to others, even in times of need. This self-imposed isolation compounded the stress and made the situation nearly unmanageable. The physical and emotional toll was immense, and I found myself completely drained, unable to focus effectively on either my work or my mother's care.

Eventually, I realized the significant mistake I had made. By refusing to delegate tasks at work and not asking for help in managing my personal crisis, I had taken on an unsustainable burden. This experience became a profound life lesson for me. It taught me the importance of recognizing my limitations, seeking support when needed, and understanding that asking for help is not a sign of weakness but a practical and necessary step in navigating life's challenges.

This difficult period reshaped my perspective. I learned that trying to shoulder everything alone is neither effective nor healthy. Delegating responsibilities and leaning on others, when appropriate, can provide the clarity and strength needed to face life's most daunting challenges.

Here, I've given 20 ways to set boundaries while maintaining the above said commitments based on my personal learning. I'm sure; these detailed explanations drive you to work on setting necessary boundaries diligently.

1. Define and Communicate Priorities

If you're working on an important project with a deadline, communicate with family that you'll be unavailable for a few hours each evening for the next week. Let them know you'll spend dedicated time with them once the project is complete.

2. Schedule "Me-Time"

Block an hour every morning for exercise or journaling. Tell your friends and family this is your self-care time and not to disturb you unless it's an emergency.

3. Set Office Hours

Let colleagues know you're available for meetings or calls from 9 a.m. to 4 p.m. (Depends on the work timing) after that, you dedicate time to family. Politely decline after-hours requests unless it's urgent.

4. Say "No" Without Guilt

If a friend asks you to help them move on a weekend you've set aside for rest, politely explain that you've committed that time to recharge and offer an alternative day if possible.

5. Use Technology to Your Advantage

Mute work-related group chats during family dinners. Similarly, turn off personal notifications during work hours to focus.

6. Create Physical Boundaries

Set up a home office space and let family members know that when the door is closed, you're focusing on work and should not be disturbed.

7. Practice Active Listening

During family dinner, put your phone away and give your full attention to your loved ones. This ensures they feel valued even when your time is limited.

8. Establish Clear Expectations

Inform your friends that while you value their company, you can only meet once or twice a month due to work and family responsibilities. Make the time together meaningful.

9. Delegate and Ask for Help

If you're overwhelmed at work, ask a colleague to collaborate on a task. At home, ask your partner or children to help with chores, freeing up time for personal pursuits.

10. Review and Adjust Boundaries Regularly

If your work schedule changes, sit down with your family and update them on how this affects your availability. Adapt your personal commitments accordingly to maintain balance.

11. Limit Unnecessary Commitments

If co-workers often ask you to join casual after-work hangouts, kindly decline when you're feeling overwhelmed and explain you need to spend time with family or rest.

12. Set Social Media Limits

Decide to check social media only during lunch breaks and after dinner, ensuring your work and family time remain uninterrupted.

13. Block Distractions

During work hours, use apps like Focus Mode to block non-work-related notifications so you can complete tasks more efficiently and free up time for family and friends.

14. Commit to Quality over Quantity

Instead of attending every extended family event, prioritize important ones, like your nephew's graduation, and spend meaningful one-on-one time with others later.

15. Practice Assertiveness

If a co-worker repeatedly assigns tasks beyond your role, firmly but politely say, "I don't have the capacity to take on additional tasks right now."

16. Define Emergency Situations

Let friends know that you won't reply to texts or calls during work unless it's an emergency, like a health issue or urgent matter.

17. Reserve Weekends for Personal Time

Dedicate one weekend day entirely for family outings or personal hobbies. Inform others you're unavailable for work or social calls during this time.

18. Use Buffer Time between Commitments

Schedule a 30-minute break between work and dinner with family. Use this time to decompress so you can transition smoothly and be fully present.

19. Protect Sleep Schedule

Set a bedtime and communicate with everyone that calls or messages after 10 p.m. will be answered the next day unless urgent.

20. Acknowledge and Respect Others' Boundaries

If a friend or family member says they're unavailable for a chat, respect their boundary. This sets a mutual understanding, encouraging them to respect yours as well.

Practical Steps to understand responsibilities while maintaining personal boundaries:

Step 1: Responsibility Map: Draw a circle in the centre of a page and write "Me." Around it, create smaller circles for your key responsibilities (e.g., family, work, friends, and community). Reflect on whether any responsibility feels overwhelming.

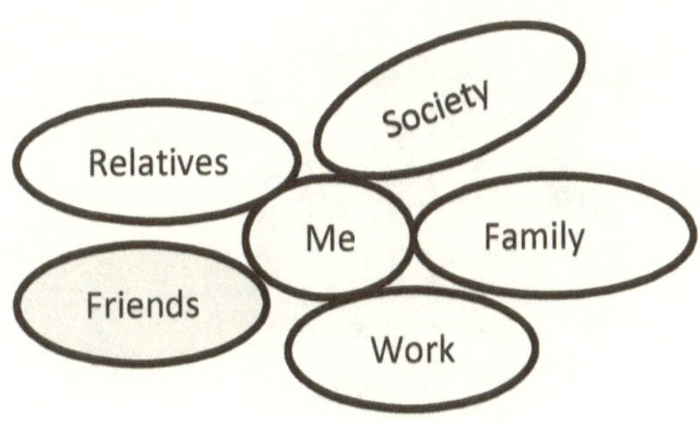

Step 2: Boundary Practice: Write one sentence you can use to assert your boundaries. Practice using it in real situations.

Example:

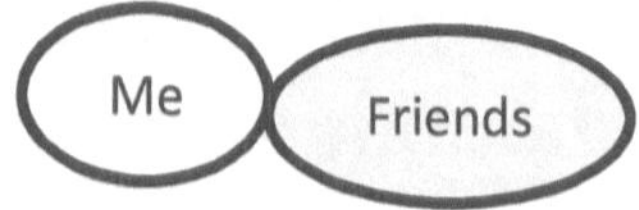

Instead of ignoring messages and calls, tell your friends politely "I really value having you in my life, and I always enjoy our conversations. I'm going through a bit of a tough time personally right now, and I may not be able to reply as much as I usually do. I hope you know it's nothing to do with you—I just need a little time. Thank you for being an amazing friend you are."

This act will subtly create more bonds between you and your friend.

Spin Continues....

Chapter 5

Chakra 4 – The Surrender (Letting Go of Control)

This chapter explores the journey toward understanding the surrender and shares insights from moments where letting go brought clarity and growth, emphasizing the power of acceptance.

Life often presents situations that test our resilience and capacity to adapt. One such transformative lesson understands that not every battle needs to be fought and not every situation controlled. This realization, while challenging, can lead to profound clarity and personal growth.

In my professional journey, as an HR professional, a pivotal moment taught me this lesson. I was entrusted with a significant opportunity—an on-site visit to Sydney for a high-stakes project. The selection was recognition of my subject matter expertise and years of experience. I was thrilled when my manager verbally confirmed my travel opportunity. However, just as I was gearing up for the role, I discovered that the manager had instead chosen a colleague—a recent addition to the team, still unfamiliar with the full process, but a close friend of the manager. It was a clear case of favouritism overshadowing expertise. Initially, I was deeply disheartened. The decision felt unjust, and I grappled with a surge of frustration and disappointment. Yet, instead of engaging in a futile battle or allowing resentment to consume me, I chose to let go. I recognized that some situations are beyond our control and fighting them can drain our energy without yielding positive outcomes.

Rather than dwelling on the setback, I used the time that would have been spent on the project to focus on my professional development. I enrolled in advanced HR certification courses, attended workshops, and honed skills that further solidified my expertise. This proactive approach not only enriched my knowledge but also opened doors to new and more fulfilling opportunities in my career.

In hindsight, what seemed like a setback became a stepping stone. By letting go, I gained the clarity to prioritize what truly mattered—my growth and my integrity. This experience reinforced a vital truth: acceptance is not about surrendering to circumstances; it's about channelling energy toward what we can control and emerging stronger from challenges.

The journey of acceptance is one of empowerment. It reminds us that every experience, even those marked by disappointment, has the potential to shape us into better, more resilient individuals.

Practical Steps to cultivate acceptance and trust in life's flow:

Step 1: Breathing Meditation: Focus on your breath for 5 minutes. Each time a thought of control arises, let it go with your exhale.

Step 2: Release Ritual: Write down something you're struggling to control on a piece of paper. Tear it up or burn it safely while saying, "I release what I cannot control."

Spin Continues....

Chapter 6

Chakra 5 – The Transformation (Embracing Change)

This chapter delves into the necessity of change as a fundamental part of life's vyugam. Covers personal transformations—both big and small—and how each change created a new foundation for self-awareness and wisdom.

Change is an inevitable part of life's journey—a constant force that shapes our paths, even when it feels unwelcome. It often challenges our desires, taking us away from what we hold close to heart, only to guide us toward new horizons of growth and understanding.

As a young girl, I dreamed of a life surrounded by my parents, siblings, childhood friends, and the comfort of my native land—a world filled with love, peace, and joy. Like many, I wished to hold onto these treasures, at least until life's natural transitions, like marriage, brought change. But destiny had other plans for me.

At the tender age of 14, I had to leave everything I cherished—my parents, my home, and the friends who felt like family. It was not a choice but a circumstance beyond my control. I found myself in a different place, living with my grandmother. Though she cared for me with love, the absence of my parents, my friends and the warmth of my native land left a void in my heart. I felt as though I had lost the world I knew and loved.

Despite the ache, I resolved to focus on my education and career. I poured my energy into building a future, even as the longing for my family and the life I left behind lingered in the background. The journey was not easy, but over time, I learned to accept this transformation as part of my life's story.

Life, however, has its own way of weaving miracles into our struggles. As the years passed, the pieces I once lost slowly returned to me. I was reunited with my loved ones, rediscovered the bonds I thought had faded, and even found a deeper connection to my roots.

During my final year of Bachelors, I faced a pivotal moment that tested my ability to step out of my comfort zone. As part of our academic requirements, I was offered the opportunity to undergo in-plant training at a prestigious organization located in Bangalore. This training was a significant milestone for students, offering invaluable exposure and experience. Many of my friends had struggled to secure approval for this training from both the college and the company, and it was considered a life-changing opportunity.

However, when the time came, I initially refused to take it up.

Coming from an orthodox family and a highly protective background, I had never been allowed to travel or stay away from home. At that young age, I was sensitive to various factors, including food habits, changes in climate, and unfamiliar environments. I also took a long time to connect with new people, which made the idea of adapting to a completely new setting even more daunting. These challenges, coupled with the fact that I was living with my grandmother at the time, made it difficult to gain her understanding and approval for the trip. As a result, I almost gave up on the opportunity, resigning myself to the belief that it wasn't meant to be.

However, my friends refused to let me miss out. They recognized the importance of this opportunity and were determined to help me overcome the hurdles. They came to my house, spoke to my grandmother, and even reached out to my parents, who were in my native town. After a lot of convincing and assurance, they managed to secure permission for me to travel to Bangalore for the training. I will always be grateful for their persistence and support, as it marked the beginning of an unforgettable experience.

When I finally arrived in Bangalore, I realized just how challenging it would be to adapt to the new environment. True to my fears, I faced difficulties from the very beginning. I fell sick due to food poisoning, struggled with homesickness, and found it hard to adjust to the unfamiliar climate. Despite these challenges, I had to report to the office every day without taking a single leave, as missing out was not an option. Through all this, my friends once again became my pillar of support. They took care of me, ensured I was able to keep up with the training, and offered constant encouragement. Their kindness and companionship made a world of difference.

Looking back, that month-long training turned out to be a transformative experience. It taught me how to adapt to new environments, deal with discomfort, and push through challenges. Beyond the technical knowledge and skills I gained, it helped me grow as an individual, equipping me with resilience and confidence that I carry to this day.

Had I allowed my initial fears and circumstances to hold me back, I would have missed out on a life-changing opportunity—a wealth of learning and personal growth. This experience stands as a testament to the importance of taking chances, even when the path ahead seems daunting, and to the incredible value of having supportive friends who believe in you.

This journey taught me that change, no matter how painful or challenging, is often the foundation for something greater. It is through change that we grow stronger, wiser, and more resilient. The transformations we endure shape us, creating space for new joys and deeper appreciation for life's blessings.

Practical Steps to adapt to and embrace life's inevitable changes:

Step 1: Change Timeline: Create a timeline of significant changes in your life. For each event, write down one positive outcome that arose from the change.

Step 2: Daily Affirmation: Repeat: "Change brings growth, and I embrace it with an open heart."

Spin Continues....

Chapter 7

Chakra 6 – The Connection (Love, Compassion and Forgiveness)

Life's journey is rarely a solitary endeavour. It is deeply intertwined with the connections we forge, the kindness we receive, and the empathy we extend. Compassion and forgiveness are not just virtues; they are bridges that link our hearts to others, fostering resilience and hope during life's most challenging phases.

Compassion is the simple yet profound act of recognizing another's pain and offering support. It reminds us that we are never truly alone. In moments of struggle, even the smallest gestures of kindness—a listening ear, a comforting word, or an offer of help—can serve as lifelines. Compassion has a ripple effect; the kindness we give often inspires others to do the same, creating a cycle of positivity that touches countless lives.

Forgiveness, on the other hand, is an act of liberation. It frees us from the weight of anger, resentment, and bitterness, allowing us to heal and move forward. Forgiving others, or even ourselves, can be one of the most difficult yet rewarding steps we take. It requires humility, strength, and an understanding that perfection is unattainable, both in others and in us. Forgiveness transforms wounds into wisdom, teaching us to grow through pain rather than remain trapped by it.

Human connections play an irreplaceable role in shaping who we are. There are moments in life when we feel lost, weighed down by challenges we cannot face alone. In such times, the presence of others— friends, family, mentors, or even strangers—acts as a guiding light. Their support can help us navigate the darkness, offering fresh perspectives and renewed strength.

For instance, consider a time when a friend extended their hand during a personal crisis. Their empathy and understanding likely provided not just solace but also a sense of direction. Similarly, a mentor's advice during a career setback might have illuminated a path forward, transforming a moment of despair into an opportunity for growth.

During my Bachelors journey, one moment stands out as a turning point that shaped my life. It was the day of the final exam of my last semester—the exam that would determine whether I would graduate.

I have always been the kind of student who absorbs everything during study holidays, storing it all in my neurons, and relying on quick revisions before the exam. But this time was different. The final semester had taken a toll on me. I had poured all my energy into our major project, which, though successful, left me completely drained—physically and mentally.

Our schedule was relentless. After completing two elective exams, I had no break before the last one, the most crucial exam of all. This exam wasn't just another hurdle; it was the key to my career. Yet, I felt utterly unprepared. Exhaustion had set in, and my usual strategy of revision seemed impossible.

The pressure was immense. I found myself overwhelmed by self-doubt, unable to focus, and battling severe back pain and a pounding headache. In that vulnerable moment, I broke down in tears in front of my mom. I told her I had decided not to appear for the exam because I didn't believe I could clear it. My confidence was shattered, and I felt defeated.

But my mom, with her quiet strength and unwavering belief in me, became my anchor. She listened to my fears without judgment and comforted me in a way only a mother could. She applied pain balm to ease my physical discomfort, spoke words of encouragement that soothed my troubled mind, and reminded me of the resilience she had seen in me time and again. Most importantly, she believed in me when I couldn't believe in myself because she had seen my preparations during study holidays.

With her support, I found the courage to step into the exam hall, despite my doubts. I gave it my best, unsure of what the outcome would be. To my astonishment, not only did I pass, but I scored an incredible 85% in that final elective.

Looking back, I realize that my mom was the game changer in that pivotal moment. Her love, trust, and encouragement became the force that pushed me forward when I was ready to give up. That day, she taught me that even in our weakest moments, the faith and support of someone who truly believes in us can work miracles. It's a lesson I carry with me to this day, and her unwavering support remains one of the greatest gifts of my life.

Love is often referred to as a universal language, a sentiment that transcends cultural, linguistic, and societal barriers. However, it is unfortunate that many people misunderstand its essence and misuse it for personal gain, often without considering the profound impact this can have on another person's life. In any meaningful relationship, the cornerstone is the mutual exchange of powerful positive emotions like love, affection, care, and forgiveness. These feelings must flow reciprocally; if they are one-sided, they lose their significance and can cause imbalance in the relationship.

Love and similar emotions may appear trivial or easily accessible until we truly experience them. The universal truth remains: whatever you give, you receive manifold. When shared sincerely, these emotions have the power to nurture and strengthen connections, creating bonds that are enduring and fulfilling.

However, relationships are not devoid of challenges. Misunderstandings and conflicts are inevitable, but how we approach and resolve them determines the longevity and quality of the relationship. When disagreements arise, it is crucial to engage in open and honest communication. Sitting down together to discuss the issue, sharing each person's perspective, and validating the importance of each point of view are essential steps. By understanding each other's feelings and concerns, you create space for empathy and resolution.

Avoid making assumptions or jumping to conclusions based solely on your own understanding. Decisions made in isolation, without involving the other person, often lead to further misunderstandings and may even result in the breakdown of the relationship. Instead, seek clarity through direct conversations; this not only resolves the issue at hand but also strengthens the foundation of trust and mutual respect.

You might wonder: What should you do when people are unwilling to engage in direct communication despite multiple requests for their time to discuss an issue? My approach is simple: after two follow-ups, let it go. Any relationship should be mutual, and if there's no response after two attempts, it's a clear sign to move on.

Life is a precious and singular journey, one that becomes richer when lived with positive emotions and meaningful connections. Cherish your relationships by aligning with love, care, and understanding. When you share these emotions, you invite your loved ones to resonate with your frequency, creating a life filled with harmony and joy.

These stories are not just personal; they are universal. They remind us of the profound impact human connections have on our lives. Acts of empathy, no matter how small, can create profound shifts in someone's journey. They reinforce the idea that while pain and struggle are inevitable, they are also temporary—so long as we lean on the support of others and extend the same to those in need.

In the end, compassion, forgiveness, and human connections teach us the most important lesson of all: we are all interconnected. Our shared humanity is a source of strength, a wellspring of hope, and the foundation for a life of meaning and purpose. Through these connections, we learn to heal, grow, and carry forward the enduring legacy of kindness and understanding.

Practical Steps to deepen your connection with yourself and others:

Step 1: Compassion Journal: Write down one act of kindness you did each day. Reflect on how it made you feel.

Step 2: Forgiveness Meditation: Sit quietly and bring to mind someone you need to forgive (including yourself). Say internally: "I forgive you, and I release the weight of this pain."

Spin Continues....

Chapter 8

Chakra 7 – The Resilience (Strength through Adversity)

Life is full of ups and downs, and every person faces hardships and setbacks at some point. These challenges can seem overwhelming, but they often teach us the most valuable lessons. When we endure difficult times, we learn more about ourselves, our strengths, and what truly matters in life. These lessons stay with us, shaping us into stronger and wiser individuals.

Resilience is the ability to recover and grow stronger after facing difficulties. It doesn't come naturally to everyone, but it can develop over time as we face challenges head-on. Each obstacle we overcome adds another layer to this inner strength, much like forging steel—heat and pressure make it tougher. Similarly, our experiences with hardship make us more resilient; helping us face future struggles with greater confidence.

When we deal with setbacks, we learn to adapt, problem-solve, and keep moving forward despite fear or failure. These experiences show us that life doesn't stop for anyone, and finding ways to bounce back is essential. Over time, this resilience becomes like a shield—a protective barrier that allows us to navigate future challenges, or "Vyugams," without being completely broken by them.

Resilience also teaches us empathy and patience. As we endure our struggles, we understand the pain and challenges others might face, making us kinder and more compassionate. Hardships, then, not only build our strength but also help us connect with others on a deeper level.

Life, at every stage, has been a remarkable teacher of resilience. But the most profound lesson in perseverance came when I was just 14 years old, during my 10th-grade year—a critical phase for any student shaping their future academic journey.

The year began with promise, as I was blessed with exceptional academic guidance from my school and teachers. However, fate had other plans. I struggled to harness their support due to a cascade of challenges that overwhelmed me emotionally and physically.

It all began early in the academic year when I lost my beloved aunt, someone incredibly close to my heart. She passed away in another city, and I travelled to bid her a final goodbye. The grief consumed me, and I couldn't return to school for a week. Just as I was trying to find my footing again, life threw another curveball—my mother had to undergo a surgery in a distant city, and I had to step into a supportive role. Her absence, coupled with the worry for her well-being, weighed heavily on me. I felt myself slipping further behind in my studies, and the hopelessness was palpable.

Before I could recover from these emotional blows, my health took a severe turn for the worse. I contracted chickenpox, and the illness ravaged me for nearly a month. I was bedridden, isolated, and disconnected from school during this critical period. By the time I recovered, I had missed weeks of lessons, vital training sessions, and the momentum I desperately needed to prepare for the upcoming board exams.

When the time came to sign the hall ticket, a wave of anxiety washed over me. Attendance was mandatory, and I had been absent for an extended period. I braced myself for rejection, knowing no school would likely overlook such a prolonged absence. But in this dark hour, my school and teachers (Two of my science teachers came to visit me at my home) proved to be nothing short of angels. Understanding my circumstances, they went above and beyond to support me.

What truly moved me were my friends—those extraordinary souls who became my lifeline. They visited me at home, brought my lessons to life, and patiently taught me all the concepts I had missed. Their unwavering support gave me hope and a sense of belonging. I can never forget my class teacher, who sent two friends living nearby to ensure I signed my hall ticket and exam forms.

Just when I thought the worst had passed, another storm hit. During the board exams, I fell severely ill with typhoid. The memories of sitting in the exam hall, battling fever and nausea, remain etched in my heart. I vividly recall the invigilator's kindness—she comforted me, encouraged me, and ensured I completed the exam despite my condition.

This relentless series of adversities, all packed into one year, tested me in ways I never imagined. At such a tender age, I experienced despair, fear, and exhaustion that could have easily derailed me. Yet, with the grace of God and the love and kindness of those around me, I persevered. My teachers, friends, and even the invigilator stood as my pillars of strength when I had little to draw from within myself.

Amazingly, despite these hurdles, I managed to complete my 10th-grade board exams with distinction. This achievement wasn't just mine—it was a testament to the collective effort, empathy, and resilience of everyone who supported me during that tumultuous time.

Though my mother couldn't be by my side then, I found a family in my teachers and friends. This year remains unforgettable—a year that taught me resilience, not in theory but through lived experience. It became the foundation of strength I continue to draw upon in every challenge life presents.

In the end, resilience is not about avoiding difficulties but about learning how to face them with courage. The more we endure and overcome the stronger and more prepared we become for whatever life throws our way. This strength, built through persistence and hard work, becomes a guide that helps us move forward, no matter how tough the journey may be.

Practical Steps to build inner strength through challenges:

Step 1: Gratitude in Adversity: Think of a recent challenge. Write down three things you learned or gained from the experience.

Step 2: Anchor Practice: Identify a physical or mental anchor (e.g., a mantra, a deep breath, a friend/mentor who heal your pain with their positive words) to return to during stressful moments.

Spin Continues….

Chapter 9

Chakra 8 – The Wisdom (Integrating Lessons Learned)

This chapter brings together the cumulative wisdom from previous chapters, reflecting on how each chakra, each battle, and each lesson contributes to a more integrated and resilient self and discusses the concept of wisdom as a constant, evolving journey.

Wisdom is often viewed as the summit of human growth—a place where knowledge, experience, and insight converge. However, wisdom is not a destination but an on-going journey, shaped and refined by every challenge we face and every lesson we learn. This concept is vividly illustrated when we reflect on the cumulative wisdom gained from the metaphorical chakras, battles, and lessons of life.

The "Chakra of Wisdom" is a conceptual metaphor that represents the continuous process of learning, growth, and self-reflection. In this metaphor, wisdom is symbolized as a Chakra that perpetually turns, each revolution representing an accumulation of knowledge, insights, and experiences that lead to personal and collective enlightenment. This cycle of learning and integrating lessons learned is not linear but rather spirals outward, growing ever broader and deeper, allowing the individual to make sense of their experiences and apply them in meaningful ways.

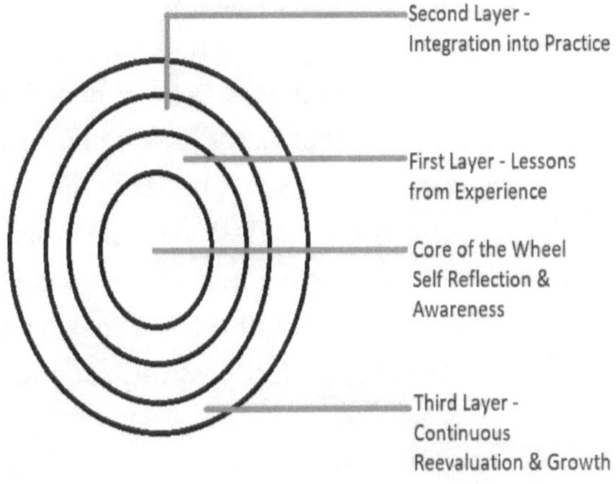

The Core of the Chakra: Self-Reflection and Awareness

At the centre of the Chakra of Wisdom lies self-reflection. Before we can truly learn from our experiences, we must first become aware of them. Self-reflection acts as the starting point for this continuous cycle. It's about being in tune with our thoughts, emotions, and behaviours, and observing how they align with or diverge from our goals, values, and beliefs. This awareness is essential because it helps us recognize when we've learned something important and when we might need to adjust our perceptions or actions.

The First Layer: Lessons from Experiences

The outer rim of the Chakra of Wisdom represents the lessons learned from our experiences. Life's challenges, successes, mistakes, and breakthroughs each contribute to the shaping of our wisdom. Every event, whether positive or negative, carries a lesson, even if that lesson isn't immediately apparent. By reflecting on each experience with an open mind and heart, we can distil valuable insights that guide our future decisions and interactions. This first layer of the Chakra is about actively seeking and acknowledging lessons, not just passively experiencing life.

This layer emphasizes the importance of a mind-set that embraces growth. It's not enough to face an experience; we must also strive to understand what that experience can teach us. A failure, for example, can be an invaluable teacher if we approach it with curiosity rather than self-criticism. Similarly, success teaches us how to build upon our strengths, provided we remain humble and thoughtful about what led to that success.

The Second Layer: Integration into Practice

Once lessons have been learned, they must be integrated into our practices and behaviours. This is where wisdom transforms from knowledge into action. It's one thing to understand a lesson intellectually, but it is a different, deeper process to embody it in our daily lives. The second layer of the Chakra of Wisdom is about translating our reflections and insights into tangible, consistent actions. It's about using what we've learned to guide our choices, inform our judgements, and shape our interactions with the world.

For example, someone who has learned the importance of patience through a challenging situation may practice taking deep breaths before responding in moments of stress. An individual who has gained insight into the value of empathy may consciously work to listen more intently when others speak. These shifts are subtle but profound, indicating that the lessons learned are no longer just ideas, but integrated into the fabric of whom we are and how we live.

The Third Layer: Continuous Re-evaluation and Growth

Wisdom is not static; it is a dynamic force that demands continual re-evaluation. The third layer of the Chakra of Wisdom represents this process of growth and adaptation. As we continue to experience life, our understanding deepens, and we may find that past lessons evolve or expand. What was once seen as a simple lesson may now reveal more intricate layers, or new experiences may offer new perspectives that challenge our previous conclusions.

This continuous re-evaluation ensures that wisdom does not become rigid or out-dated. It is through this layer that we learn to navigate change with resilience and adaptability. The Chakra's movement allows us to grow not only through the challenges we face but also through the feedback we receive from others and the broader world. The wisdom we accumulate becomes increasingly nuanced as we consider it in light of new experiences and deeper understanding.

Openness and humility are fundamental in the process of integrating wisdom. Being open means allowing ourselves to question long-held beliefs and embrace new perspectives. Humility, on the other hand, allows us to recognize that we do not have all the answers and that there is always more to learn. This humility ensures that we do not become complacent in our wisdom but remain open to the possibility of change, growth, and deeper insights.

A key aspect of integrating lessons learned is the willingness to admit when we have erred and to seek wisdom from others. When we are humble in our approach to wisdom, we see it as a communal process—one that involves listening, sharing, and growing together. This openness to others' experiences and knowledge is essential, as it broadens our understanding and reinforces the idea that wisdom is a shared resource, not an individual pursuit.

The beauty of the Chakra of Wisdom lies in its interconnectedness. Each experience, lesson, and insight is a thread woven into the larger fabric of our understanding. The Chakra is not segmented into isolated parts; instead, it is an organic whole in which each layer influences the others. The wisdom gained in one area of life often reverberates through other areas. For instance, learning to manage stress effectively in one part of life can improve relationships, decision-making, and even creativity in others.

This interconnectedness also suggests that wisdom is not confined to one's personal experience. It draws from a rich tapestry of human knowledge, culture, and history. The lessons we learn are shaped by those around us, as well as by the collective wisdom of humanity. By embracing this interconnectedness, we expand the capacity of the Chakra of Wisdom to guide not just individuals, but communities, organizations, and societies.

One of the most profound elements of the Chakra of Wisdom is its cyclical nature. Just as a Chakra turns and returns to its starting point, so does wisdom. Each cycle brings us closer to a deeper understanding, yet each new revolution reveals that there is always more to learn. As we move through life, we may revisit similar lessons, but each time, the context changes, offering new opportunities for growth.

The cyclical movement of the Chakra is a reminder that wisdom is a lifelong journey, not a destination. It encourages us to approach each phase of our lives with an open mind, a willingness to learn, and recognition that even in our later years; we can still discover new insights that enhance our understanding of the world and ourselves.

The Chakra of Wisdom is a powerful metaphor for understanding how we learn, grow, and integrate lessons into our lives. Through self-reflection, embracing experiences, integrating lessons into action, and maintaining openness to continuous learning, we build a deeper and more expansive understanding of ourselves and the world. The cyclical nature of the Chakra teaches us that wisdom is not a final goal, but an on-going process—one that enriches our lives, enhances our relationships, and allows us to live with greater purpose and clarity.

Practical Steps to Reflect on life's lessons and use them as guides.

Step 1: Lesson Reflection: Choose one life experience and ask yourself:

- What did I learn?
- How has this lesson shaped me?

Step 2: Teaching Others: Share one lesson you've learned with someone else.

Spin Continues....

Chapter 10

Chakra 9 – The Final Chakra (Finding Peace within the Vyugam)

This Chapter discusses the idea of harmony in accepting the presence of vyugams. Rather than trying to eliminate challenges, and explores how one can find inner peace by accepting life's cycles as a continuous source of growth.

Life is a dynamic interplay of experiences, emotions, and events that weave together a narrative unique to each individual. Central to this narrative are the cycles, or vyugams, that punctuate our existence. Vyugams represent the challenges, transitions, and phases that shape our journey through life. These cycles, often perceived as obstacles, are in fact essential for growth and transformation. This discussion explores the concept of finding peace within the vyugams, emphasizing the need for acceptance, mindfulness, and a deeper understanding of life's intrinsic rhythms.

The important aspects to find peace when facing the inner battles are:

- Understanding the rhythm of Life
- Acceptance - The gateway to peace
- Mindfulness – Anchoring in the present moment
- Growth through Challenges
- Cultivating Inner Harmony
- The Interconnectedness of all things

Understanding the Rhythm of Life:

The term vyugam encapsulates the cyclical nature of life—a pattern observed in every aspect of existence. Just as the seasons change, the tides ebb and flow, and the moon waxes and wanes, human lives are marked by periods of joy, sorrow, success, failure, health, and illness. These cycles remind us that no state, whether desirable or challenging, is permanent. Yet, our instinctive reaction to vyugams often involves resistance, denial, or an attempt to escape the perceived discomfort they bring.

Resistance arises because challenges disrupt the equilibrium we seek. The uncertainty and discomfort accompanying a difficult phase can provoke anxiety, frustration, and a sense of powerlessness. However, this resistance only intensifies our suffering. The act of fighting against these natural rhythms isolates us from the deeper lessons and opportunities for growth inherent within them. To find peace, we must first acknowledge and embrace the inevitability of vyugams.

Acceptance: The Gateway to Peace:

Acceptance is not synonymous with resignation. It is an active, intentional practice that requires courage and humility. By accepting the presence of vyugams, we shift our perspective from resistance to openness. This openness allows us to view challenges as integral components of life's design rather than as deviations or punishments.

When faced with adversity, acceptance begins with acknowledging the reality of the situation without judgment. This acknowledgment does not negate the difficulty of the experience but rather creates space for us to process our emotions and respond thoughtfully. For example, during a period of personal loss, accepting the pain as a natural expression of love and attachment can provide solace. It allows us to grieve fully while understanding that this phase, too, will pass.

Acceptance also involves letting go of the illusion of control. Life's cycles often unfold beyond our influence, and resisting them only compounds our distress. By releasing the need to control every aspect of our journey, we cultivate a sense of surrender—not to defeat but to the wisdom of life itself. This surrender fosters a profound sense of peace, rooted in trust and faith in the unfolding process.

Mindfulness: Anchoring in the Present Moment

Finding peace within vyugams requires us to anchor ourselves in the present moment. Mindfulness, the practice of cultivating awareness of the here and now, is a powerful tool for navigating life's cycles. It allows us to observe our thoughts, emotions, and sensations without being swept away by them.

During challenging phases, mindfulness encourages us to acknowledge our pain without becoming consumed by it. For instance, if we are experiencing anxiety, mindfulness invites us to explore the sensation without judgment or resistance. By doing so, we create a space where the anxiety can exist without overwhelming our sense of self.

Mindfulness also enhances our ability to appreciate the fleeting joys of life. In moments of happiness, it reminds us to taste the experience fully, knowing that it is part of a larger, ever-changing cycle. This balanced approach to both pleasure and pain fosters equanimity—a state of inner calm that persists regardless of external circumstances.

Growth through Challenges

Vyugams are not merely hurdles to be endured; they are profound opportunities for growth and transformation. Challenges force us to confront our limitations, question our assumptions, and reassess our priorities. They compel us to develop resilience, adaptability, and inner strength.

Consider the metaphor of a seed. To grow into a tree, the seed must endure the darkness of the soil, the pressure of the earth, and the unpredictability of the elements. Similarly, humans must navigate the dark and difficult phases of life to emerge stronger and more self-aware.

Each challenge carries within it the seeds of wisdom. A period of professional failure, for example, can teach humility, patience, and the value of perseverance. A health crisis may prompt us to re-evaluate our lifestyle and prioritize well-being. By embracing these lessons, we transform adversity into a catalyst for positive change.

Cultivating Inner Harmony

Inner harmony is the natural outcome of accepting and embracing life's vyugams. It arises from the understanding that life's cycles are not separate from us but are integral to our being. This harmony is nurtured through practices that connect us with our inner selves, such as meditation, journaling, and introspection.

Meditation provides a sanctuary of stillness amidst the turbulence of vyugams. It allows us to detach from the external chaos and connect with the unchanging core of our being. Journaling helps us process our experiences, articulate our emotions, and gain clarity. Introspection encourages us to examine our thoughts and beliefs, fostering self-awareness and acceptance.

Community and support also play a vital role in cultivating harmony. Sharing our experiences with trusted individuals or groups reminds us that we are not alone in our struggles. The collective wisdom and compassion of a supportive community can provide strength and encouragement as we navigate our cycles.

The Interconnectedness of All Things

Finding peace within vyugams also involves recognizing the interconnectedness of all life. Our individual cycles are part of a greater whole—a universal rhythm that unites all beings. This awareness fosters a sense of humility and gratitude. It reminds us that just as we experience challenges, so does every living entity. By embracing this shared experience, we develop empathy and compassion for ourselves and others.

The interconnected nature of life also teaches us that every phase, no matter how difficult, has its purpose. Just as the winter prepares the earth for spring, our challenges prepare us for new beginnings. Trusting this process allows us to approach life with hope and resilience.

Finding peace within vyugams is not a destination but a continuous journey. It is a process of learning to dance with life's rhythms rather than resisting them. By embracing acceptance, practicing mindfulness, and seeking growth, we transform challenges into opportunities for deeper understanding and fulfilment.

Ultimately, peace within vyugams is rooted in our ability to align with the natural flow of existence. It is a state of being that transcends the dualities of joy and sorrow, success and failure. In this state, we discover not only serenity but also the profound beauty and wisdom inherent in every cycle of life.

Practical Steps to achieve harmony by embracing life's cycles.

Step 1: Cycle Visualization: Imagine life as a turning wheel, with ups and downs. Reflect on how each phase contributes to the whole.

Step 2: Gratitude Practice: Every night, write down three things you're grateful for, recognizing the completeness of each day.

Step 3: Meditation: Sit in silence and repeat: "I am one with the cycles of life. I find peace in every turn."

Spin Continues....

Chapter 11

Conclusion

Beyond the Chakra – Life's Infinite Lessons

"Beyond the Chakra- Life's Infinite Lessons" is an exploration of the deeper, often hidden teachings that life offers, framed through the metaphor of the wheel. A Chakra is a simple, everyday object, but it holds profound symbolic weight in many cultures and philosophies. It represents the cycle of life, the constant motion forward, the endless rotation of experiences, and the evolution of the self. The phrase "Beyond the Wheel" suggests looking past the surface of life's routines, challenges, and mundane repetitions to uncover the deeper wisdom these cycles impart.

The wheel, in its simplest form, revolves around a central axis. This axis can be likened to the core of our being—the self, our values, beliefs, and essence. Just as a Chakra cannot turn without its hub, life cannot move forward meaningfully without a strong sense of inner purpose. We are often caught in the rotations of daily tasks, moving from one event to the next, yet within this cycle, we are constantly given the opportunity to learn and grow.

One of the first lessons beyond the Chakra is the importance of balance. A Chakra that is imbalanced will wobble and veer of course, just as our lives, when out of balance, tend to feel chaotic. Life's infinite lessons often teach us the need to find equilibrium—between work and rest, action and reflection, ambition and acceptance. The Chakra teaches us that these opposites are not at odds with each other but are necessary to maintain movement, to stay on track. Understanding this balance can be transformative, allowing us to experience a more harmonious existence.

Another lesson is the concept of impermanence. Wheels are always in motion, constantly turning, never static. Similarly, life is in constant flux. Nothing is permanent, and each moment gives birth to the next. Life's infinite lessons often revolve around the idea of accepting change—whether in ourselves, our relationships, or the world around us. Holding on too tightly to the past or fearing the unknown future causes suffering. Accepting change, as the Chakra accepts its rotation, allows us to move forward with grace.

Moreover, the Chakra represents cycles—of seasons, relationships, challenges, and growth. It is a reminder that life moves in circles. We often find ourselves revisiting situations, people, or emotions, thinking we are stuck in repetition. But these cycles are not a sign of stagnation; they are opportunities to refine ourselves, to approach challenges from a new perspective. Just as the Chakra turns and brings us to the same point, we may return to the same challenges or lessons, but each time, we bring with us new wisdom and a deeper understanding.

Another vital lesson beyond the Chakra is the need for resilience. A Chakra endures pressure, friction, and wear with every rotation. It faces obstacles, yet it continues to roll forward, adapting to the terrain. Life's infinite lessons often challenge us to embrace resilience in the face of hardship. We, too, face moments of difficulty, suffering, or loss, but it is through these struggles that we learn our true strength. Just as a Chakra must be strong to serve its purpose, we must cultivate an inner resilience to navigate life's challenges.

The Chakra also reflects the idea of interconnectedness. A wheel, with all its spokes working together, operates as one unified system. In the same way, we are all interconnected, part of a larger network of relationships, communities, and the universe itself. Our actions, thoughts, and energy ripple outward, affecting others and the world. Life's infinite lessons teach us that our lives are not isolated; they are deeply interwoven with the lives of others. Understanding this interconnectedness encourages empathy, compassion, and a sense of shared responsibility for the well-being of all.

Lastly, beyond the Chakra lies the understanding that life is a journey, not a destination. Just as a Chakra is always moving, the essence of life is in the movement itself. The lessons we learn are not always about reaching a particular goal or achieving success, but rather about growing through each experience. It is the process; the turning of the Chakra that defines us. Embracing this journey with all its twists, turns, and bumps is where the deepest wisdom is found.

"Beyond the Chakra- Life's Infinite Lessons" ultimately teach us that life is a continuous, evolving journey of growth, learning, and transformation. By embracing balance, impermanence, resilience, interconnectedness, and the constant flow of life, we are able to transcend the surface and uncover the deeper truths that guide us toward a more meaningful existence. Each turn of the Chakra brings us closer to understanding ourselves and the world, leading us to infinite opportunities for learning, healing, and evolving.

Of course, the spin continues, naturally, until our final moment ....

Key Points for Our Neurons to Remember:

1. Everything you seek lies just beyond your fear and hesitation.

2. True transformation begins the moment you step outside your comfort zone.

3. If something is truly meant for you, life will present it twice—it's up to you to seize it.

4. Your intuition is a divine whisper, always guiding you toward the right path.

5. Honest and direct communication is the foundation of strong and lasting relationships.

6. That which troubles you the most is the very thing destined to foster your growth.

7. People will interpret your story through their own lens, but remember—how they treat you is merely a reflection of themselves.

8. Don't believe everything others say—find out the truth by yourself. It becomes clear only when you see it with your own eyes, without being influenced by others' opinions.

9.Whether it's career, money, relationships, friendships, or material possessions—if something is truly meant for you at a soul level, life will find a way to bring it back, even after years apart. Our logical mind may not recognize the deep desires of the soul, but the universe always does.

10. Many times, overthinking holds us back from taking the next step. Instead, focus on positive possibilities and move forward—you'll be amazed at the magic that unfolds.

11. The world mirrors our energy—give love, and love finds its way back to you.

12. Even your shadow abandons you in the dark, but one truth stands strong—you are your only constant.

May this wonderful life fulfill all that your soul longs for!

Thataasthu!!!

A Note of Gratitude to My Readers

Dear Reader,

As you turn the pages of this book, you've become more than just a reader to me—you've become a companion on this journey. Writing Chakra Vyugam - Lessons from Life's Inner Battle was not just an act of storytelling but an unveiling of my soul. It was an offering, a bridge between my heart and yours. And for choosing to walk this path with me, I am deeply grateful.

Thank you for lending your time, your mind, and your spirit to this work. In today's fast-paced world, where every moment is a precious choice, your decision to engage with my words is a gift I do not take lightly.

To me, this book is more than ink on paper; it is a mirror reflecting the universal struggles, lessons, and triumphs we all face in our inner battles. The fact that you chose to delve into these reflections, to hold space for the ideas, and to interpret them in your own unique way, fills my heart with profound gratitude.

Your willingness to explore, to question, and perhaps even to transform, breathes life into these pages. Without you, these words would remain static, mere thoughts bound by silence. But with you, they take on a new dimension—a shared connection, an exchange of meaning.

Thank you for your open heart, your curious mind, and your willingness to embark on this journey. Whether this book has resonated deeply or sparked just a fleeting thought, know that it has found its purpose because of you.

With every word I've written, I hoped to touch your soul. And with every word you've read, you've touched mine. For that, I am eternally grateful.

With all my heart,

Deepiga S

Join me at

Instagram - @inked_With_Optimism